Vo Trong Nghia

Vo Trong Nghia / Building Nature

Volume 02 : Bamboo / *with an introduction by* **Philip Jodidio**

with 180 illustrations

Contents

Connecting People with Nature / *Philip Jodidio*

With the growth of cities around the world and the pressures of looming climatic catastrophe, architecture should be called on to transform itself from a source of pollution to a reason for hope. Nor is this idea anecdotal: the World Green Building Council estimates that 39 per cent of energy-related carbon emissions can be attributed to buildings. An awareness of architecture's responsibilities has permeated many circles of the profession in the developed world, while new forms, ideas and solutions are beginning to emerge from elsewhere, including places where these issues are most acute.

Since 1986, Vietnam has been transitioning from a centrally planned system to a market economy. Prior to pandemic-related issues in 2020, the annual GDP growth of the country approached 7 per cent, with about 8 per cent of a total population of nearly 100 million below the poverty line. Although population growth slowed after the 1990s, urban centres such as Ho Chi Minh, with around 9 million people (21 million in the larger metropolitan area) and a density of 4,292 people per square kilometre as of 2019, pose problems for architecture. The tropical climate places issues of building design differently here than in much of the rest of the world. Ho Chi Minh, surprisingly,

has only 0.7 m² (8 sq ft) of green area per resident, compared to Tokyo, which has 10.6 m² (108 sq ft).

Vietnam has yet to emerge as a leading country in contemporary architecture, in part because of its long recovery from decades of war (the First Indochina War, from 1946 to 1954, and the Vietnam War, 1955 to 1975). Vo Trong Nghia was one of the first Vietnamese architects to gain international notoriety. He was born in Quang Binh province, near the border between North and South, one year after the end of the Vietnam War. 'When I was young, I remember only eating rice and fish sauce,' he says. 'This continued until I was 20 years old, when I went to Japan. My village only got electricity in 1996, which had its drawbacks, but I didn't have TV, so that was good.'

Vo traces his desire to become an architect from a simple story. 'One day an architect came to my village, and I saw that he appeared to be rich,' he says. 'Since my family was poor, I thought that if I became an architect, I would also be rich. That was honestly my first thought – very simple, very naive, and it would appear that I was wrong.'

Huong An Vien Welcoming House, Hue

He adds that at the time, the only way to engage in advanced studies for architecture was to go abroad. Vo received a Japanese government scholarship and studied at the National Institute of Technology, Ishikawa College, and then the Nagoya Institute of Technology, where he graduated with a Bachelor of Architecture degree in 2002. He got his Master's degree in Civil Engineering from the Landscape and Civic Design Laboratory, University of Tokyo, in 2004, and was the recipient of the university's Furuichi Award for his thesis on wind and water. Vo studied under Hiroshi Naito, a well-known minimalist architect who had worked with Fernando Higueras in Madrid and Kiyonori Kikutake in Tokyo, and has observed: 'The purpose of architecture is for the people. I'm not very interested in the work of star architects. These appear like buildings from outer space.'

Vo Trong Nghia's academic success in Japan and his open spirit speak to his talents, and announced an unusual itinerary. 'I planned from the outset to stay there for ten years,' he says, 'because I think you need that much time to learn architecture. Before I went to Japan, I imagined there would only be high-rise buildings. I was wrong, they protect their forests very well. They harvest wood for architecture in a responsible way.

In the cities, the gardens are very small, but the Japanese adapt nature to these circumstances – for example, with bonsai trees. We can learn a lot from the way they design courtyards. They are the best in the world for that scale of architecture.'

As well as absorbing a great deal of knowledge about Japanese architecture, Vo came across another impetus for his future career while in Tokyo: a book about the Colombian architect Simón Vélez, who was a proponent of bamboo architecture with its large spans, and high, voluminous spaces and domes. But the younger architect immediately looked further: 'As I read the book, I felt that I could do better. Vélez used a lot of steel joints, which are costly and do not look nice.'

Vo returned to Vietnam, and in 2006 founded Vo Trong Nghia Architects in Ho Chi Minh. One of his first completed projects, the Wind and Water Bar (2008; p. 24) in Binh Duong province, makes clear reference to his sources and influences. The building sits on an artificial lake and has an open, semicircular form, built entirely from bamboo. Of this project, the studio notes: '[It] uses the principles of aerodynamic design. Computer simulations of the spaces were used to study the air flow and

Naman Retreat, Da Nang

the cooling capacity of the water. These studies allowed us to reduce the use of electrical energy, such as air-conditioning, lowering the building's energy costs.'

In contrast to the adjacent café, the Wind and Water Bar is an enclosed, flexible space. A structural arch system supports the 10 m (33 ft)-high, 15 m (49 ft)-wide dome, and the main frame is made up of forty-eight prefabricated units, each comprising several bamboo elements that are bound together. Wind energy and water from the lake create natural ventilation, and a 1.5 m (5 ft)-wide hole at the top of the roof allows the evacuation of warm air. 'The building has a luxurious feeling,' Vo says, 'but at the same time remains gentle in its atmosphere. The bar is also used for town meetings and other social activities. The two buildings – café and bar – originated from nature, and now merge in harmony with nature. With time, they will return to nature.'

Another of the architect's early works is Bamboo Wing (2009; p. 36) located in Vinh Phuc province, near Hanoi, a pure bamboo structure that features an open space, 12 m (39 ft) in height, for concerts, weddings and other ceremonies. 'The structure takes the form of a bird's wings and floats over the landscape of its site,' Vo explains. 'With its deep eaves and the surrounding water, people feel as if they are living in nature.' Although this type of building seems to be closely related to Vietnam, he says, 'bamboo was used for baskets or small home items, but not for architecture. Maybe I was the first in Vietnam to use bamboo for buildings.'

Vo has continued to build in bamboo since coming to international attention in the 2000s, but has also created numerous 'green' buildings, the focus of the first volume. The links between these two aspects of his designs are clear – they are joined together by a deep connection to nature. 'The ways that we design bamboo structures and introduce plants into our green buildings are different, but I think my ideas are the same,' he says. 'Architects often tend to destroy nature, but we find a way to save it. If we build too much, we will destroy the ecosystem. Through architecture, I still want to protect our planet and reintroduce greenery into the city. We should use bamboo when we can – for cafés, restaurants, even schools or pavilions.'

His approach and logic are fundamentally unusual, and run counter to many of the currents of contemporary architectural practice. Rather than admitting that architecture is ephemeral by nature, Vo posits the contrary. 'We try to create buildings

opposite, above *Nocenco Café, Vinh*
opposite, below *Wind and Water Bar, Binh Duong*

that can last for two or three hundred years and to convince every client to agree,' he says. 'People talk about sustainable architecture, but in reality the life of buildings is too short. In large Asian cities, buildings date back just a few decades, but look very old and ugly. If you want to build again, you have to destroy nature and start over. The first condition of sustainability is that buildings need to have a long life. We do not have many old buildings in Vietnam, so it is important that when we build, those structures should have a long life.'

Nor does he admit that architecture made from bamboo cannot be made to last: 'Bamboo can be smoked a little every few years. This is an ancient technique to avoid insect infestation. Like other types of timber, bamboo can last for a long time if it is well maintained. We design our bamboo buildings like machines, with parts that can be replaced if necessary.'

Vo does admit, however, that his bamboo designs may have some geographical and climatic limits. 'We have done work in China where the climate is colder,' he says. 'I would say that the kind of work we do can exist in places with temperatures that go down to 0° C (32° F), but perhaps no colder. Bamboo is fine for South East Asia or India, as well as parts of China.'

He explains the direction of his architectural designs in terms that demonstrate the breadth of his approach and ambition: 'We focus on connecting people with nature, and try to make a small mark on the city. In Vietnam, our cities have so few parks. People are being taken away from nature for the moment. That's why we have conflict everywhere in the world – without nature around us, we become crazy. Because there has been so much war in Vietnam, we have not been able to develop a modern tradition of architecture. I wanted to create a way of designing that harmonized with nature – using simple and cheap materials, without the need for air-conditioning – and a new language of architecture for Vietnam.'

Hiroshi Naito's idea of architecture for the people comes to mind when approaching the work of Vo Trong Nghia – increasingly so, as the scope and range of his work expands. Vo connects his thought process and work methods directly to his Buddhist faith and his personal search for enlightenment, a welcome change from the 'starchitects' shunned by Naito. In fact, recent developments in Vo's career and his own statements make clear just how unusual and significant an architect he is.

Bamboo Stalactite, Venice Biennale

Projects

02.1_

Wind and Water Bar / *Binh Duong, Vietnam*

The Wind and Water Bar in Binh Duong province is a pure bamboo structure – the first such building designed by the studio. Stepping stones lead guests across an artificial lake and then into the bar, which is also used for cultural events and social gatherings. In contrast to the open, linear space of the adjacent café, the bar was designed as a closed dome, so that the project as a whole ended up with two very different types of buildings, with the café blending in and the bar standing boldly out from its surroundings.

The aim of the design was to celebrate local crafts, as well as to create green architecture for the modern age. For the dome, a structural arch system was designed, 10 m (33 ft) in height, with a span of 15 m (49 ft). The main frame comprises forty-eight units, each one assembled from various lengths of bamboo, which were bound together and bent into arches. Dividing the structure into prefabricated units made it possible to realize an accurate

building within budget, and assembling them on site allowed for more flexibility in transportation. Other passive design methods included the creation of natural ventilation by harnessing wind energy, and designing a circular opening at the top of the ceiling to release the hot air generated below – all of which helped to reduce the building's overall energy consumption.

Projects like the Wind and Water Bar and the adjoining café offer low-cost investment and rapid assembly – the bar was built by local workers over a three-month period – as well as the potential for reduced energy consumption, both during construction and throughout its lifetime. Essentially, the bar was born from nature, then joined in harmony with nature, and will eventually be returned to nature.

The dining area, looking up to the skylight

above *The bamboo frame of the dome*
opposite *The frame seen from the outside*

The dome under construction

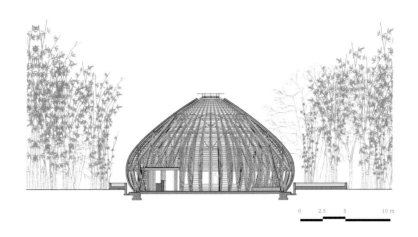

0   2.5   5   10 m

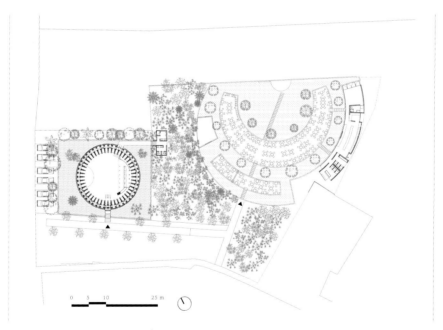

0   5   10   25 m   ↻

top *Section*
above *Site plan*
opposite *Details of the bamboo joints*

above *Access to the first floor from the seating area*
opposite *View up to the skylight*

02.2_

Bamboo Wing / *Vinh Phuc, Vietnam*

Set in idyllic natural surroundings in Vinh Phuc province, near Hanoi, Bamboo Wing is a cantilevered structure that hangs in the air like a pair of outstretched bird's wings. The aim of the project was to study bamboo not only as a finishing material, but also as a structural one, and to cultivate the potential space that could be created with it. The building, at 12 m (39 ft) wide, is balanced on supports at the rear, without columns at the front, which allows ample space for hosting fashion shows, conferences, concerts and other cultural events.

The only structural materials used in the project were bamboo and stainless steel wires, to help reinforce the roof against storms. The construction process created a new trend for using ecological materials that were readily available throughout Vietnam. The bamboo was treated using traditional methods, rather than chemicals, by soaking it in mud and then smoking it to make it antiseptic and mothproof. Finally, the bamboo was heated to create the ideal curvature.

Internal and external finishes were also made from natural, locally sourced materials, including stone for the walls, which was quarried near the site, and thatch for the roof. All of the auxiliary facilities – kitchen, storage areas and lavatories – were covered with earth and planting to form little hills that merge into and become part of the peaceful landscape.

The shape of the roof was designed specifically to bring the breeze from the pond into the building, and the deep eaves cast shadows on the floor, ensuring a comfortable thermal environment without the need for air-conditioning. Together, the use of natural materials such as bamboo and stone, along with water and open spaces, have created a venue in which visitors feel as if they are in peaceful harmony with nature.

The bamboo frame, running along the curve of the structure

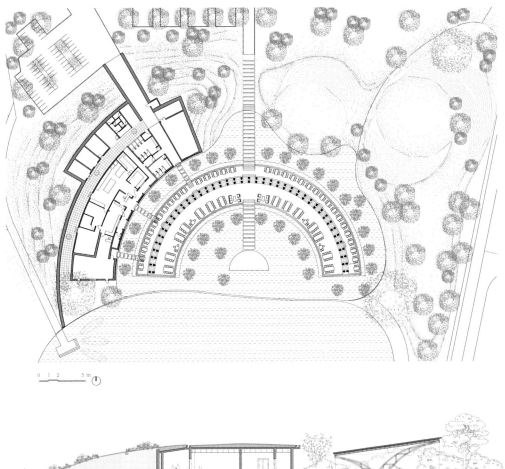

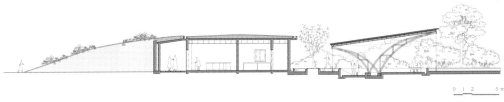

0 1 2   5 m

0 1 2   5 m

top *Site plan*
above *Section*
opposite, above *Exterior view*
opposite, below *View of the pond between the restaurant and service area*

Looking out from the seating area to the elevated outdoor platform

The bamboo frame, seen in the dining area

above *View from the pond*
opposite *The entrance at night*

Dai Lai Conference Hall / *Vinh Phuc, Vietnam*

The residential complex Flamingo Dai Lai Resort was intended to cater for busy city dwellers who wanted to escape from their daily existence in cramped apartments and enjoy their weekends while being surrounded by nature. It sits in a beautiful woodland setting between Dai Lai Lake and the mountains, about 50 km (31 miles) from Hanoi.

The Dai Lai Conference Hall is located beside the main access road to the resort, where an impressive curved stone wall along the road guides guests into the complex. The wall – 80 m (262 ft) in length, 8 m (26 ft) high and 1 m (3 ft) thick – provides a sequential view, revealing and screening the landscape as visitors progress along it, tempting them inside, before they eventually enter through an orthogonal access point between artificial hills to reach a foyer covered with a dynamic bamboo structure of extraordinary dimensions.

The structure of the conference hall itself comprises straight poles of bamboo. Bamboo as a building material has many advantages, from its beautiful colour and texture to its reproduction potential. The poles were assembled into a structural frame, with a maximum span of 15 m (49 ft), and the position of each joint was adjusted to allow a generous curve for the roof. The functional requirements of the centre meant that it had to be divided into separate rooms – including a main hall, a smaller hall, a foyer and supporting rooms – but the space creates the impression that the rooms are larger and more open. The sense of continuity is enhanced via a transom window above the partitions.

Bamboo and stone are abundant in the area, and the design made the most of these local materials to create an original building with a special atmosphere. As a result, the conference hall is a friendly accompaniment to the landscape, one that not only offers a pleasant space for events, but also deepens visitors' experience of the generous spirit of the outdoors.

Exterior view of the conference hall

The conference hall against a backdrop of mountains

View towards the entrance from the public grounds

above *Looking down to the rear of the hall*
opposite, from top *Section, plan and front elevation*

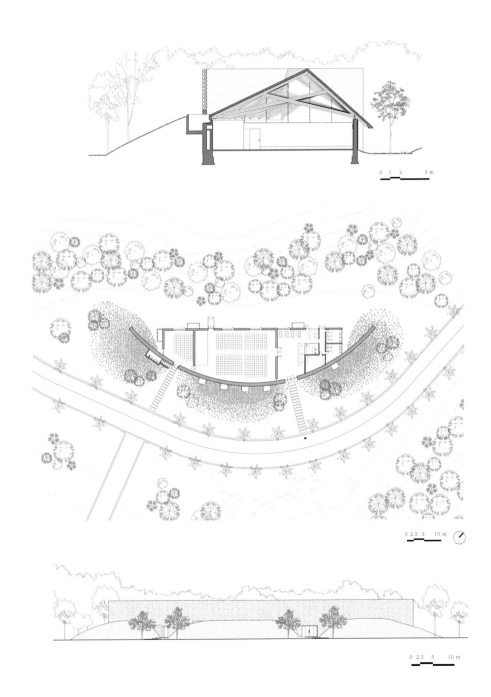

0 1 2   5 m

0 2.5 5   10 m

0 2.5 5   10 m

above *View from the reception area to the outside*
opposite *Details of the joints and connections to the thatched roof*

above *The seating area*
opposite *The curved bluestone wall, extending to the bamboo ceiling*

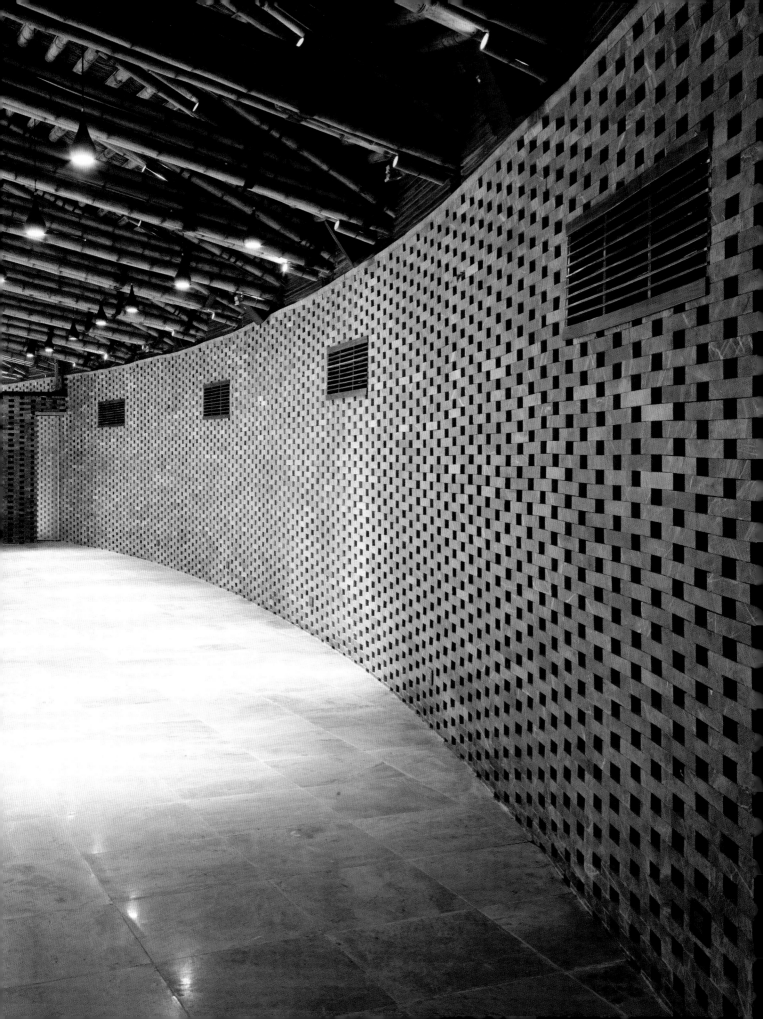

02.4_

Kontum Indochine Café */ Kon Tum, Vietnam*

Occupying a corner plot next to the Dak Bla Bridge, the Kontum Indochine Café is part of a hotel complex in the city of Kon Tum, in the Central Highlands of Vietnam. Along with catering for hotel guests, it also functions as a semi-outdoor banqueting hall for weddings. The café comprises two elements: a main building with a large bamboo roof structure, and an annex kitchen made from concrete and stone. The main building is rectangular in plan, and is surrounded by a shallow artificial lake. All of the elevations open to the outside: to the south, the building faces the main street along the Dak Bla River; to the east, the service street; to the west, a restaurant and banquet building belonging to the hotel; and to the north, the annex kitchen.

By providing shadow beneath the bamboo roof and maximizing the flow of cool air from the lake, the indoor space is able to dispense with air-conditioning, even in a tropical climate. The roof is covered with thatch and translucent fibre-reinforced plastic panels, and supported by a pure bamboo structure comprising fifteen cone-shaped units. The shape of these units was inspired by the traditional Vietnamese fishing basket, which narrows gradually from the top to the base. From the café, guests can enjoy a panoramic view of the mountains and the Dak Bla River, framed by the bamboo arches. The columns create the impression of being in a bamboo forest, and connect visually with the mountains beyond.

The challenge of the project was to respect bamboo as a material and to create a distinctive space. Its characteristics are different from timber or steel. If the details and construction methods of buildings made from those materials are applied to structures made from bamboo, its advantages may be impaired. Using steel joints, for example, undermines bamboo's cost benefits, as they generate too much load, which can cause buckling.

Here, we used traditional methods (soaking in mud and smoking) to treat the bamboo, along with low-tech joint details (rattan ties and bamboo nails), which are more suitable for bamboo structures. The columns were prefabricated before being put in place to achieve the required quality and accuracy.

The cone-shaped bamboo columns at night

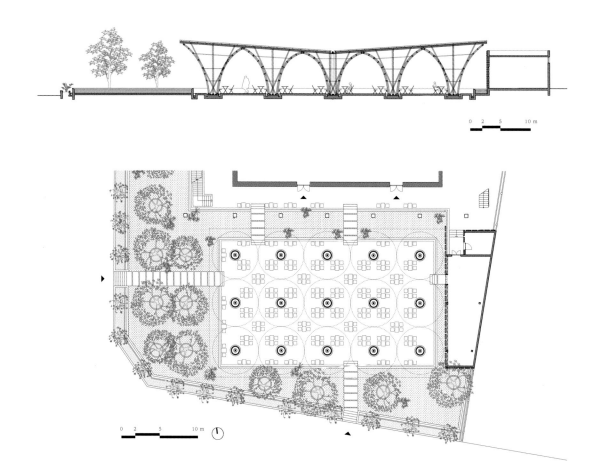

above *Section and plan*
opposite, above *Front view*
opposite, below *Side view towards the pond and bamboo columns*

above *View from the entrance*
opposite *Seating area along the bamboo columns and pond*

02.5_

Son La Restaurant / *Son La, Vietnam*

Son La province in northwestern Vietnam is an area of outstanding natural beauty with untouched forests and mountainous landscapes. But even with its strong cultural heritage, there was little development or accommodation to lure tourists to the region. Son La Restaurant, which can accommodate 750 guests, is the first facility of a new hotel complex located near the city centre to maximize this potential.

The difficult terrain means that Son La is only accessible from Hanoi via a seven-hour car trip along precarious cliff roads, making the transportation of building materials and work crews difficult. The project, therefore, needed to make the most of local resources, including labour and affordable materials such as bamboo and stone.

The tropical monsoon climate means that it is very hot with high humidity and strong rains in the wet season, and more temperate but still hot in the dry season. To accommodate these extremes of weather, the building comprises eight separate stone buildings and an open-air bamboo dining zhall. The buildings have multiple entrances to the dining hall and framed views out to the external dining area, and their varying heights together with the trees on the roof

create a vertical landscape. The stone for the walls was sourced a mere 10 km (6 miles) from the site, and provides texture and connection with the surrounding landscape.

To build the roof structure, we used a local type of bamboo (*luong*), which grows to 8 m (26 ft) in height. Ninety-five columns, comprising four bamboo poles each, create the feeling of being in a bamboo forest. The poles, with a diameter of 8 to 10 cm (3 to 4 in.) each, were assembled using bamboo nails and rope after being treated in the traditional way by soaking in mud and then smoking. Shear loads were braced by ten layered and crossed bamboo beams, connected to the stone buildings. For the ceiling, we used local thatch (*vot*), with transparent composite roof sheeting. Skylights between the columns flood the space below with soft light. Finally, hundreds of peach trees were planted in the grounds.

The project was built on a modest budget of approximately US $600/m². The restaurant forms the entrance to a sustainable hotel complex, which will eventually include a conference hall and café, forming a cultural centre for locals and future tourists.

The bamboo columns, with connections to the ceiling

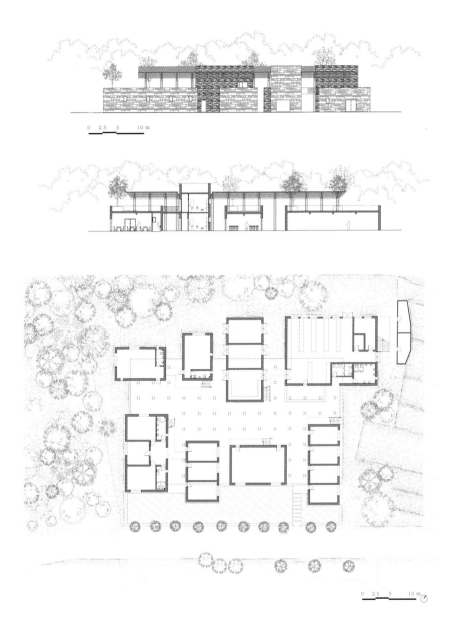

0   2.5   5   10 m

0   2.5   5   10 m

above, from top *Elevation, section and plan*
opposite, above *Exterior view*
opposite, below *View of the ceiling and the supporting bamboo columns*

above *View of the seating area*
opposite *Details of the bamboo columns and joints*

above *Dining tables sit between the bamboo columns*
opposite *The interior at night*

02.6_

Son La Ceremony Dome / *Son La, Vietnam*

Son La Ceremony Dome is part of a hospitality complex designed by the studio, which includes the Son La Restaurant (pp. 74–85), in Son La, a culturally diverse area in the Central Highlands of Vietnam that is surrounded by mountains and dense vegetation. This building was designed as a new space to accommodate the increasing numbers of visitors to the area.

Because bamboo is a familiar local material and easy to obtain, it was used for the main structure of the restaurant, the first project in the complex to be realized, which became instantly recognizable to locals and a symbol of the city. Here, bamboo was also used to make the five dome structures, their differing heights creating a 'skyline' that took inspiration from the mountains and the peaceful wooded landscape.

The largest dome, at 15.6 m (51 ft) in height and 283 m^2 (3,046 sq ft), contains a café. The four other domes – two at

12.5 m (41 ft) in height and 227 m^2 (2,443 sq ft), and two at 10.5 m (34 ft) in height and 164 m^2 (1,765 sq ft) – will serve as a foyer and reception area for welcoming guests, as well as being multipurpose spaces for outdoor celebrations, parties and ceremonies. The domes have a double-layered structure and thatched roofs; a skylight on the top of each allows natural light and ventilation to penetrate inside.

The trees planted in the grounds will eventually grow taller than the domes, creating a pleasant, shaded environment over the next few years. The sounds from a waterfall and stream between the ceremonial hall and the domes also contribute to the feeling of relaxation, as does the nearby rose garden.

A bamboo frame inside one of the domes

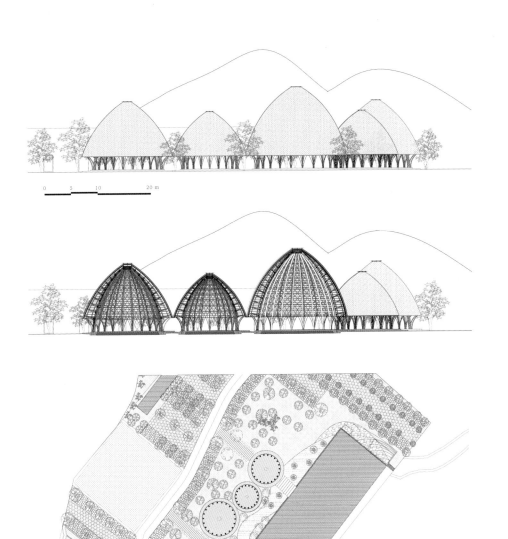

0   5   10   20 m

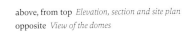

0   5   20   40 m

above, from top *Elevation, section and site plan*
opposite *View of the domes*

above *Young trees add to the feeling of serenity*
opposite *View up to the skylight*

The thatched roofs of the domes

02.7_

Nocenco Café / *Vinh, Vietnam*

This renovation project was for a café on the top floor and rooftop of a seven-storey concrete building in the city centre of Vinh, in northern Vietnam. From here, guests have a magnificent view over the surrounding houses and other old buildings, towards the river and forest. Many of the buildings in the area were damaged by the Vietnam War, and most of them have been renovated with colonial-style façades inspired by European designs – an influence that continues to this day.

The client decided not to change the envelope of the existing structure, but to instead create a unique and attractive addition that would turn the building into an urban landmark. The challenge was to create impact by inserting a new structure made from local materials. After studying various options, including brick and stone, we decided on bamboo. We knew from experience that bamboo was readily available, reducing construction time and budget, and its light weight means that

it only needs a few workers to carry it and can be easily transported to the top floor by crane. It was also possible to install the bamboo structure without any additional support.

On the top floor, we covered the existing concrete building with bamboo. Because the ceiling is also covered with bamboo, it is instantly recognizable to pedestrians on the street below. Ten bamboo columns hide the existing structure, and together with four additional columns, elegantly divide the space into various private areas. The enormous dome, housing a rooftop club, and the rectangular volumes on the roof fit into the existing L-shaped space. These volumes offer framed views of the historic stadium and the cityscape beyond, as well as connecting the two vaulted bamboo structures, which open up to the cityscape beyond.

Sunlight filters through the skylight into the interior

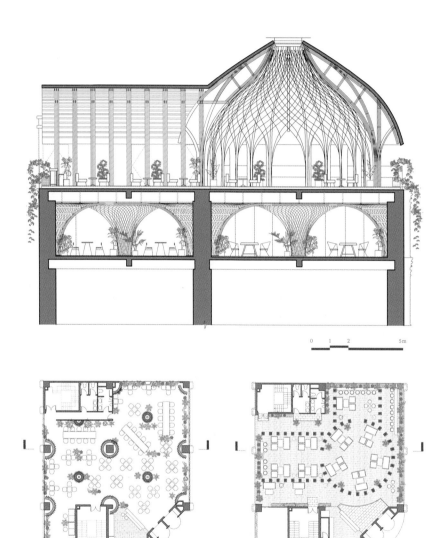

0   1   2   5m

0 1 2   5m

above *View of the café at night*
opposite, above *Section*
opposite, below *Plans*

The bamboo frame on the rooftop

View of the interior

02.8_

Bamboo Stalactite / *Venice, Italy*

Bamboo Stalactite is an installation created for the 2018 Venice Architecture Biennale. The theme that year was 'Freespace', and our design was intended as a community space that could be shared equally by everyone, which was open and free to all. Because of this sense of community, it had to be easy to realize, simple in structure and able to be produced on a low budget.

For this project, we used bamboo as the only building material. Owing to its distinctive flexibility, bamboo allowed us to realize the project with limited resources – it took just eight workers, with the support of Vietnamese and Italian architects and students, to build the pavilion in twenty-five days. This flexibility extended beyond the building itself – bamboo helps to create

a space that is rich in its connection to nature, and one that quickly becomes a landmark in the city, despite its small size.

The pavilion comprises eleven modules, each shaped by the combination of two hyperbolic shell structures. The structural beams had already been prepared in Vietnam. It can be transported easily, becoming a community space that can be replicated anywhere – in a museum, a school or in the countryside, creating a destination that is free and open to all. Its potential is limitless, and this undiscriminating quality is what we wanted our design to offer.

The frame and hyperbolic-paraboloid shell structure

above *Exterior view*
opposite, above *Elevations*
opposite, below *Plan*

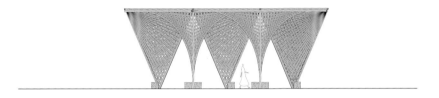

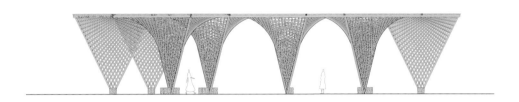

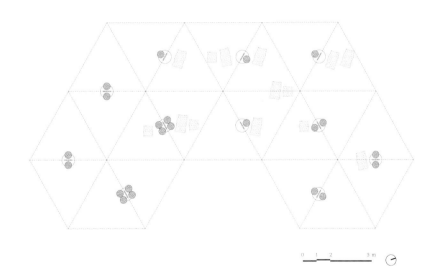

0 1 2   5 m

Detail of the bamboo shell

Close-up view of the joints

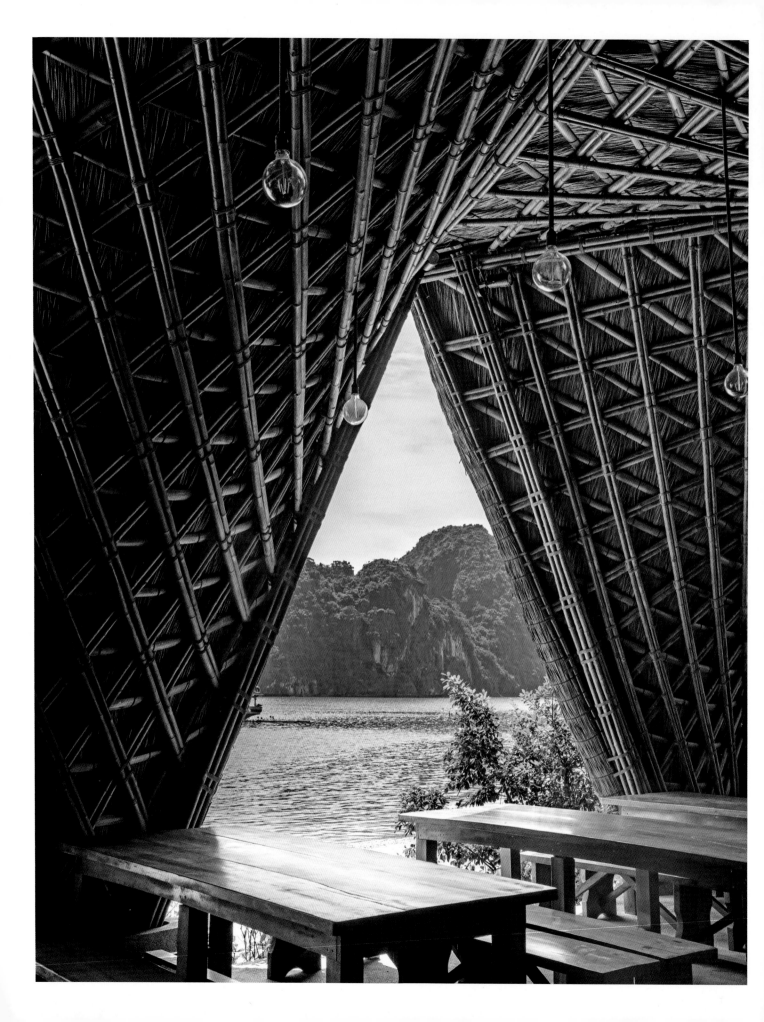

02.9_

Castaway
Island Resort / *Cat Ba Archipelago, Vietnam*

Castaway Island Resort, located on a tiny island in the popular tourist destination of Cat Ba Archipelago in northern Vietnam, is accessible only by boat, a trip that takes about two hours from the port city of Hai Phong. Bordered on one side by a mountain range and an expanse of white sandy beach on the other, the resort comprises five huts, a restaurant and an events pavilion, and can accommodate up to 160 guests.

For this project, we used bamboo because it can be integrated into its surroundings without affecting the natural beauty of the waterside setting, and can eventually be removed easily. The restaurant features a hyperbolic-parabolic (h-p) bamboo shell structure, which forms a semi-outdoor space for social gatherings. The five huts were built using bamboo frame modules, which were assembled on the ground to reduce the construction time and ensure quality. Recycled timber shutters, typically used in old colonial villas, form the façades.

And finally, the buildings were covered with traditional Vietnamese thatched roofs to reduce their environmental impact. Each of the thirteen shell units comprises eighty straight bamboo poles, creating wavy ceilings and rhythmic roof structures. Thin bamboo poles (*tam vong*), 40 to 50 mm (1½ to 2 in.) in diameter, were assembled using bamboo dowels, before being tightened with rope.

These bamboo structures not only enhance each visitor's experience while staying at the resort, but have also become landmarks within this popular tourist destination. Despite the construction process, the beauty of the site has been left intact, thanks to the use of such an environmentally friendly material – an intentionally eco-conscious approach we adapted for the project.

View out to the bay, framed by the h-p shell structure

0   5   10   20 m

above *Bird's-eye view of the complex*
opposite, from top *Elevation, site plan and floor plan*

above   *The entrance to one of the bungalows*
opposite   *View of the upper floor of a bungalow, seen from the bay*

Exterior view of the bungalows

02.10_

Naman Retreat / *Da Nang, Vietnam*

Located on the main road between Da Nang and Hoi An old town is Naman Retreat, a coastal resort 16 km (10 miles) from Da Nang International Airport.

Our aim was to design a modern but peaceful tropical resort complex that would provide spa treatments and activities such as yoga and beach sports in a friendly, welcoming environment, and to bring together the disparate elements of the 8.4-acre site, comprising eighty bungalows, six VIP villas and a further twenty villas. To achieve the perfect atmosphere in which guests can attain purification of body and mind, we used a harmonious blend of planting, stone and bamboo.

The conference hall

The conference hall, which can accommodate up to 300 people, is the first building visitors see when approaching from the reception zone. It is a rectangular structure with an asymmetrical pitched roof and vaulted bamboo ceiling, and comprises two parallel spaces: the interior hall, and an open external corridor that also serves as an outdoor lobby.

The main bearing structures are the bamboo frames, with a span of 13.5 m (44 ft) in the hall and 4 m (13 ft) in the corridor, with a ceiling height of 9.5 m (31 ft). The arches were formed using bent poles. By stepping the glass façade back into the volume, three frames of the arch structure sit outside the building, creating a foyer space.

Two different types of bamboo were used. For the straight columns, we chose *luong* bamboo for its strength and height, which can reach 8 m (26 ft), and *tam vong* bamboo for the arches because of its flexibility. The reason for selecting bamboo as the main material was that the clients wanted a flexible, large open space that could be built quickly with a modest budget and used for different functions. Because it is locally sourced and affordable, it was the ideal material. Prefabrication also allowed for a fast and efficient construction process, with more control over the entire build.

The vaulted bamboo frame system

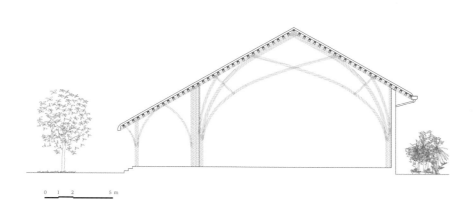

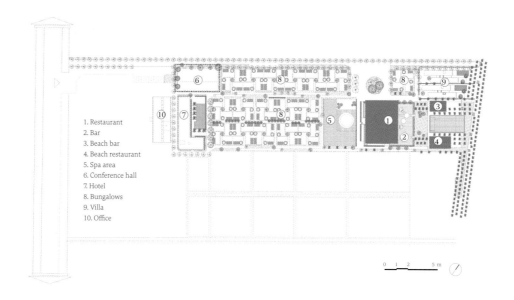

1. Restaurant
2. Bar
3. Beach bar
4. Beach restaurant
5. Spa area
6. Conference hall
7. Hotel
8. Bungalows
9. Villa
10. Office

top *Section*
above *Site plan*
opposite, above *Front view*
opposite, below *Side view*

above *Details of the bamboo frame*
opposite *The corridor at night*

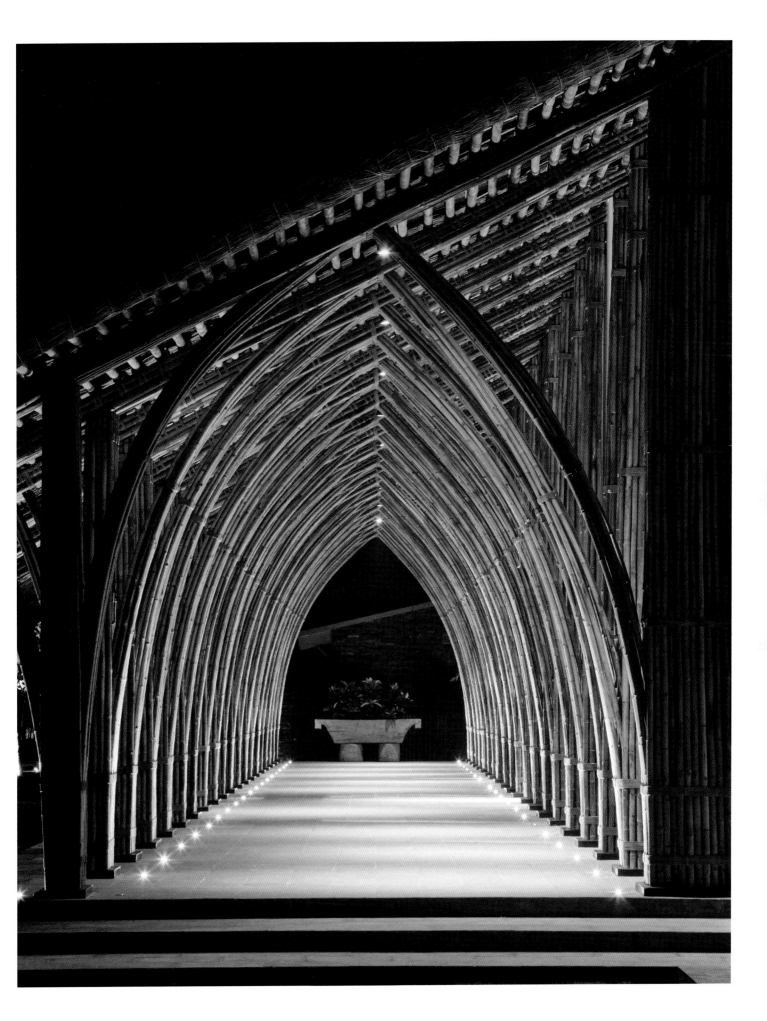

The restaurant

The restaurant, rectangular in plan and made using bamboo, overlooks the beach and swimming pool, and can accommodate 350 guests. This area is the main dining space for the complex, providing meals for both guests of the resort and visitors. A basement contains the kitchen and service spaces. The diverse range of spaces was created by changes in floor level and by the bamboo structure of the building.

Large groups can eat together beneath the two bamboo domes, with twenty-nine cone-shaped bamboo columns dividing the space further into smaller, more intimate spaces for families or couples. During the day, glass skylights at the top of each dome allow light into the dining space below. The restaurant also provides outdoor space for al fresco dining.

For the interior, we designed a glass façade supported by concrete columns to create a space that can be fully closed for air-conditioning, and yet still be connected to the outside. All of the bamboo used on site was treated naturally in situ, a four-month-long process that comprises bending by fire, soaking in water and fumigation.

The cone-shaped columns consist of straight bamboo poles (*luong*) on the inside, with an outer surface created by bent poles (*tam vong*). In order to get the most benefit from the material, the design followed the features and characteristics of each type. For large spans, *luong* bamboo is more suitable, as the poles can reach lengths of up to 8 m (26 ft), with widths of up to 100 mm (4 in.). For bending poles, *tam vong* is the perfect choice: the width is narrower, but the skin is thicker, allowing the poles to be very flexible.

opposite, above *View from the pond at night*
opposite, below *Entrance to the bamboo dome*

above *Exterior view*
opposite, above *Section*
opposite, below *Plan*

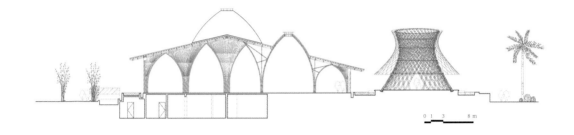

0 1 3   8 m

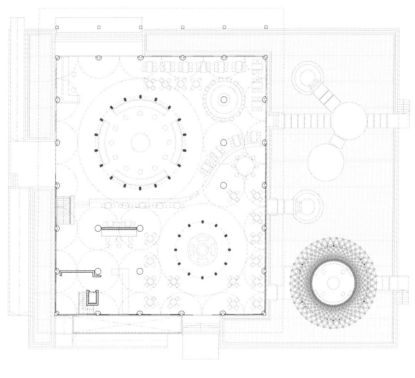

0 1 3   8 m

The bar

In front of the restaurant is a small, organically shaped building, which seems to float on the surface of the water. This building serves as the bar, and is connected directly to the restaurant. Its unusual curving shape – a hyperboloid shell – looks dynamic, but the geometry is very simple. The surface is like a cylinder, rotated in two directions. To create this twisted surface, straight poles of *luong* bamboo were used. This type of bamboo was particularly suitable, owing to its strength and height. The bar gives guests a unique experience of relaxing on the surface of the water, but also acts a buffer zone between the restaurant and the beach.

opposite, above *View of the bar*
opposite, below *The interior, showing the bamboo frame*

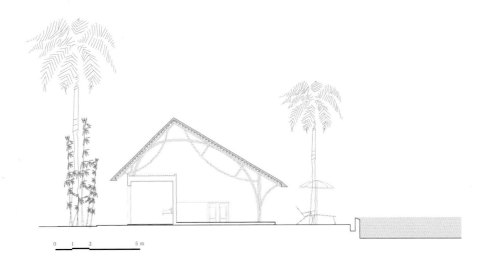

0 1 2   5 m

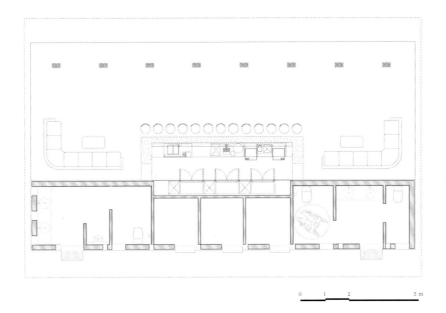

0   1   2   5 m

top *Section*
above *Plan*
opposite *Details of the bamboo frame and joints*

02.11_

Huong An Vien
Welcoming House / *Hue, Vietnam*

Huong An Vien cemetery is located in the village of An Hoa, about 10 km (6 miles) southwest of Hue city centre. At its heart is the Welcoming House, a pure bamboo structure. In response to the feelings of grief and loss associated with places like these, both client and architect set out to create an architectural form that would make the space feel lighter and more comfortable to be in.

Located on four natural lakes and surrounded by mountains, the park is also planted with numerous trees. This helps to create a rich diversity of wildlife, allowing visitors to enjoy the natural beauty of the trees and flowers. The design of the curved bamboo roof was inspired by the romance of the historic city of Hue and the Huong River. Its form creates a focal point for the cemetery, and evokes a feeling of relaxation and tranquility.

The roof curves and slopes down very low, both to shield the bamboo structure from sunlight and rain and to create a cool, friendly space with a human scale. The thatch of the roof and natural materials connect the building to its surroundings. Cheap materials that are popular locally were also used, such as breeze blocks, to create ventilation and reduce the need for air-conditioning, and increase natural light.

opposite *Exterior view*
on p. 162 *View from the lake (above) and of the bamboo ceiling (below)*
on p. 163 *Section (above) and site plan (below)*

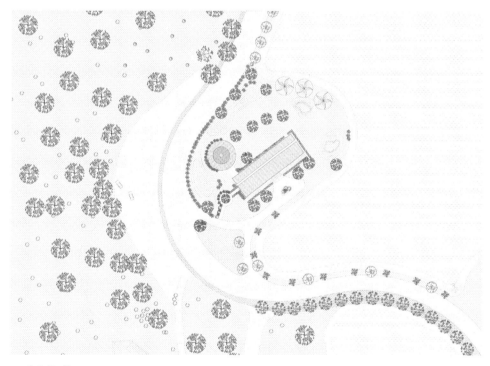

0 5 10 20 m

The bathroom opens into the circular courtyard

Pre-cast concrete blocks allow for ventilation

Project credits

02.1 Wind and Water Bar / pp. 24–35

Location: Binh Duong, Vietnam
Completed: 2008
Architects: VTN Architects
    (Vo Trong Nghia Architects)
Lead architect: Vo Trong Nghia
Architect: Ritsu Uchiyama
Programme: Bar and restaurant
Gross floor area: 270 m² (2,906 sq ft)
Site area: 1,160 m² (12,486 sq ft)
Client: Wind and Water Company JSC
Contractor: Nghiem Dinh Toan

02.2 Bamboo Wing / pp. 36–47

Location: Vinh Phuc, Vietnam
Completed: 2009
Architects: VTN Architects
    (Vo Trong Nghia Architects)
Lead architect: Vo Trong Nghia
Architects: Tran Ba Tiep, Nguyen Minh Tung
Programme: Café and restaurant
Gross floor area: 1,430 m² (15,392 sq ft)
Client: Hong Hac Dai Lai JSC
Contractor: Hong Hac-Dai Lai JSC

02.3 Dai Lai Conference Hall / pp. 48–63

Location: Vinh Phuc, Vietnam
Completed: 2012
Design: VTN Architects
    (Vo Trong Nghia Architects)
Lead architects: Vo Trong Nghia, Takashi Niwa
Architects: Dau Nhat Quang, Le Thi Anh Huyen
Programme: Conference hall
Gross floor area: 730 m2 (7,858 sq ft)
Client: Hong Hac Dai Lai JSC
Contractors: Hong Hac Dai Lai JSC,
    Wind and Water House JSC

02.4 Kontum Indochine Café / pp. 64–73

Location: Kon Tum, Vietnam
Completed: 2013
Design: VTN Architects
    (Vo Trong Nghia Architects), ICADA
    (icada.asia)
Lead architect: Vo Trong Nghia
Design team: Dau Nhat Quang
Programme: Café
Gross floor area: 551 m² (5,931 sq ft)
Site area: 1,150 m² (12,379 sq ft)
Contractor: Wind and Water House JSC,
    Truong Long JSC

02.5 Son La Restaurant / pp. 74–85

Location: Son La, Vietnam
Completed: 2014
Design: VTN Architects
     (Vo Trong Nghia Architects)
Lead architect: Vo Trong Nghia
Associate architect: Vu Van Hai
Architects: Ngo Thuy Duong, Tran Mai Phuong
Programme: Restaurant
Gross floor area: 1,984 m² (21,356 sq ft)
Site area: 2,200 m² (23,681 sq ft)
Client: Tien Doan Trading Co. Ltd
Contractor: Suoi Hen JSC,
     Wind and Water House JSC

02.6 Son La
     Ceremony Dome / pp. 86–99

Location: Son La, Vietnam
Completed: 2017
Design: VTN Architects
     (Vo Trong Nghia Architects)
Lead architect: Vo Trong Nghia
Design team: Nguyen Duc Trung
Programme: Ceremony dome
Gross floor area: 1,000 m² (10,764 sq ft)
Client: Tien Doan Trading Co. Ltd
Construction video:
     https://vimeo.com/211050558

02.7 Nocenco Café / pp. 100–11

Location: Vinh, Vietnam
Completed: 2018
Design: VTN Architects
     (Vo Trong Nghia Architects)
Interior design: VTN Architects
     (Vo Trong Nghia Architects)
Lead architects: Vo Trong Nghia,
     Nguyen Tat Dat
Design team: To Quang Cam,
     Le Hoang Tuyet Ngoc, Takahito Yamada
Programme: Café, club
Gross floor area: 687 m² (7,395 sq ft)
Site area: 438 m² (4,715 sq ft)

02.8 Bamboo Stalactite / pp. 112–19

Location: Venice Biennale, Italy
Completed: 2018
Design: VTN Architects
    (Vo Trong Nghia Architects)
Lead architects: Vo Trong Nghia,
    Nguyen Tat Dat
Architects: To Quang Cam,
    Thomas Boerendonk
Programme: Installation
Gross floor area: 290 m² (3,122 sq ft)

02.9 Castaway Island Resort / pp. 120–33

Location: Cat Ba Archipelago, Vietnam
Completed: 2019
Design: VTN Architects
    (Vo Trong Nghia Architects)
Lead architects: Vo Trong Nghia,
    Takashi Niwa
Design team: Nguyen Duc Trung,
    Nguyen Minh Khuong, Koji Yamamoto
Programme: Resort
Gross floor area: 1,100 m² (11,840 sq ft)
Client: Tung Long Trading Joint Stock Company
Contractor: Wind and Water House JSC

02.10 Naman Retreat / pp. 134–59

Location: Da Nang, Vietnam
Completed: 2015
Design: VTN Architects
    (Vo Trong Nghia Architects)
Lead architect: Vo Trong Nghia
Architects: Ngo Thuy Duong,
    Nguyen Van Thu
Programme: Restaurant
Gross floor area: Restaurant 2,124 m² (22,863 sq ft);
    Bar 100 m² (1,076 sq ft)
Client: Thanh Do Investment Development
    and Construction JSC

**02.11 Huong An Vien
        Welcoming House** / pp. 160–9

Location: Hue, Vietnam
Completed: 2020
Lead architects: Vo Trong Nghia, Nguyen Tat Dat
Design team: Le Hoang Tuyet Ngoc
Programme: Cemetery
Gross floor area: 500 m² (5,382 sq ft)
Site area: 588 m² (6,329 sq ft)

Photo credits

All plans and drawings provided courtesy of
VTN Architects (Vo Trong Nghia Architects)

All photos by Hiroyuki Oki, apart from the following:

12–13 Francesco Galli, courtesy La Biennale di Venezia;
100–11 Trieu Chien

Index

Page numbers in *italics* refer to illustrations

Thanks to Koji Yamamoto, Quang Tuan Ta and Vu Tran Huy Phi for their editorial assistance, and to Le Hien and Nguyen Hoang Tri Nhan for content editing. And special thanks to all of the staff at VTN Architects for their contribution to this book.

Vo Trong Nghia studied architecture at the Nagoya Institute of Technology and the University of Tokyo, before founding Vo Trong Nghia Architects in 2006 in Ho Chi Minh, Vietnam. His designs are at the foregront of 'green' architecture and sustainable practices, and have recieved numerous accolades, including multiple World Architecture Community Awards and a *Wallpaper* Design Award in 2021.

Philip Jodidio studied art history and economics at Harvard, and edited *Connaissance des Arts* for over twenty years. His books for Thames & Hudson include *Casa Tropical: Houses by Jacobsen Arquitetura* and *The New Pavilions*.

First published in the United Kingdom in 2022 by
Thames & Hudson Ltd, 181A High Holborn, London WC1V 7QX

First published in the United States of America in 2022 by
Thames & Hudson Inc., 500 Fifth Avenue, New York, New York 10110

Vo Trong Nghia / Building Nature – Volume 2: Bamboo
© 2022 Thames & Hudson Ltd, London
Text © 2022 Vo Trong Nghia Architects
Introduction © 2022 Philip Jodidio

Designed by Steve Russell / www.aka-designaholic.com

British Library Cataloguing-in-Publication Data
A catalogue record for this book is available from the British Library

Library of Congress Control Number 2021942696

ISBN 978-0-500-34359-3

Printed in China by RR Donnelley

MIX
Paper from responsible sources
FSC® C144853
www.fsc.org

Be the first to know about our new releases, exclusive content and author events by visiting
thamesandhudson.com
thamesandhudsonusa.com
thamesandhudson.com.au

On the cover:
Front *Castaway Island Resort, Cat Ba Archipelago*
(Photo: Hiroyuki Oki);
Back *Son La Ceremony Dome, Son La*
(Photo: Hiroyuki Oki)

On pp. 2–3 *Castaway Island Resort, Cat Ba Archipelago*
pp. 4–5 *Son La Ceremony Dome, Son La*
pp. 6–7 *Son La Restaurant, Son La*
p. 10 *Kontum Indochine Café, Kon Tum*
pp. 12–13 *Bamboo Stalactite, Venice Architecture Biennale*